Rookie Biographies®

SERENA WILLIAMS

A Champion on and off the Court

by Jodie Shepherd

Content Consultant

Nanci R. Vargus, Ed.D.
Professor Emeritus, University of Indianapolis

Reading Consultant

Jeanne M. Clidas, Ph.D.

Children's Press®
An Imprint of Scholastic Inc.

Library of Congress Cataloging-in-Publication Data

Names: Shepherd, Jodie, author.
Title: Serena Williams : a champion on and off the court / by Jodie Shepherd.
Description: New York, NY : Children's Press, an imprint of Scholastic Inc.,
[2016] | Includes index.
Identifiers: LCCN 2016002670| ISBN 9780531216842 (library binding) |
ISBN 9780531217672 (pbk.)
Subjects: LCSH: Williams, Serena, 1981–Juvenile literature. | Tennis
players—United States—Biography—Juvenile literature. | African American
women tennis players—Biography—Juvenile literature.
Classification: LCC GV994.W55 S54 2016 | DDC 796.342092–dc23
LC record available at http://lccn.loc.gov/2016002670

Produced by Spooky Cheetah Press

© 2017 by Scholastic Inc.

All rights reserved. Published in 2017 by Children's Press, an imprint of Scholastic Inc.

Printed in China 62

SCHOLASTIC, CHILDREN'S PRESS, ROOKIE BIOGRAPHIES™, and associated logos are
trademarks and/or registered trademarks of Scholastic Inc.

1 2 3 4 5 6 7 8 9 10 R 25 24 23 22 21 20 19 18 17 16

Photographs ©: cover main: Bradley Kanaris/Getty Images; cover background: titelio/
Thinkstock; 3: Pereiro/Dreamstime; 4-5: Julian Finney/Getty Images; 6-7, 10-11: Ken
Levine/Getty Images; 12-13: Caryn Levy/Sports Illustrated/Getty Images; 14: Allsport
UK/Getty Images; 15: Rick Rycroft/AP Images; 16-17: Globe Photos/ZUMAPRESS.
com/Alamy Images; 18 background-19: Cameron Spencer/Getty Images; 18 main:
Christine Chew/UPI Photo Service/Newscom; 20 background: Robert Prezioso/Getty
Images; 20 top inset: Robert Prezioso/Getty Images; 20 bottom inset: Robert Prezioso/
Getty Images; 22: SGranitz/Getty Images; 23: Luis Sinco/Getty Images; 24-25: Simon
Maina/Getty Images; 26-27: Stephane De Sakutin/Getty Images; 29: Carlos Barria/
Reuters; 30: Pereiro/Dreamstime; 31 top: Simon Maina/Getty Images; 31 center top:
Robert Prezioso/Getty Images; 31 center bottom: Globe Photos/ZUMAPRESS.com/
Alamy Images; 31 bottom: John Vachon/Library of Congress; 32: Pereiro/Dreamstime.

Maps by Mapping Specialists

TABLE OF CONTENTS

Meet
Serena Williams

Serena Williams is one of the greatest tennis players ever. But she had to overcome many **obstacles** to achieve that goal. Over the years, Serena has shown that, with talent and **perseverance**, anything is possible.

Serena Williams was born in Saginaw, Michigan, on September 26, 1981. She had four older sisters: Lyndrea, Yetunde, Isha, and Venus. Soon after Serena was born, the family moved to Compton, California.

Serena first started playing tennis when she was three years old.

The Williamses could not afford kid-size tennis rackets. Serena had to learn how to play using an adult-size racket.

CANADA

Saginaw●

UNITED STATES

■Compton

MEXICO West Palm Beach■

Area enlarged

MAP KEY

● City where Serena
Williams was born

■ City where Serena
Williams lived

The Williams family did not have much money. All five sisters shared one bedroom. There were only four beds. Serena took turns sharing with each sister. "Instead of feeling like I didn't belong anywhere, I felt like I belonged everywhere," she said.

Serena's neighborhood was not always safe. Her parents hoped tennis might help. If Serena and Venus played well enough, the family might be able to move somewhere safer. Both parents coached the girls. Soon, Serena and Venus were winning tournaments.

This photo shows Serena at tennis practice in 1992.

Serena (left), her dad, and Venus (right)

Serena Grows Up

Serena and Venus practiced every day. But their parents made sure there was still time for relaxing. Venus became a star first. She was the best tennis player in her age group in the U.S. Serena soon became the best in her age group, too.

Serena worked hard both on the court and in school. She was a very good student. Serena also won nearly every tennis match she played. She became a professional player when she was 14.

Venus (left) and Serena (right) pose with President Reagan and his wife Nancy.

Serena played at the Australian
Open in 1998. She made it all
the way to the quarterfinals!

Serena holds her trophy at the U.S. Open.

When Serena was 18, she won the U.S. Open. That is one of the most important tournaments for tennis players. Before long, she was winning major championships again and again.

FAST FACT!

Serena has been ranked the #1 women's tennis player in the world six times so far, the first time in 2002 and most recently in 2015.

Serena and Venus play doubles together as a team. They also play against each other. Serena says Venus is her best opponent! They make each other work hard. They are fierce rivals *on* the court. But they are the closest of sisters *off* the court.

Venus and Serena show off their medals at the 2000 Olympics.

Serena and Venus have won
many championships, including
three Olympic gold medals.

Serena injured her ankle at the 2013 Australian Open.

Challenges Met

Not everything was easy for Serena. She faced many obstacles. Some people did not like seeing a black player winning so many games. They shouted **racist** comments when she played.

Serena had other challenges, too. She was injured several times. During those times, she could not play at all.

In 2003, something terrible happened. Serena's sister Yetunde was shot and killed. Later, Serena started the Serena Williams Foundation in Yetunde's honor. It helps young people all over the country live better lives.

Serena posed with her sister Yetunde in 2003.

People lit candles and placed flowers in the spot where Yetunde was killed.

Serena teaches kids
in Kenya, Africa,
how to play tennis.

Working for Others

Serena has found other ways to help people, too. She teaches children in tough neighborhoods how to play tennis. Without these clinics, the kids might not have the chance to learn. She has also opened two schools in poor villages in Kenya, Africa.

Serena has also been an **ambassador** for UNICEF. This organization helps kids around the world. She does all this in between training and competing! Serena believes all children should have the chance to make their dreams come true, no matter where they live or how much money they have.

Serena (left) and Venus (right) pose with young tennis players in South Africa.

Serena Williams is a true champion. She works hard to achieve her goals. And she works to give other people the chance to achieve theirs, too!

Timeline of Serena Williams's Life

1981 > **1985** > **1995**

Born on September 26

Begins playing tennis

Turns professional

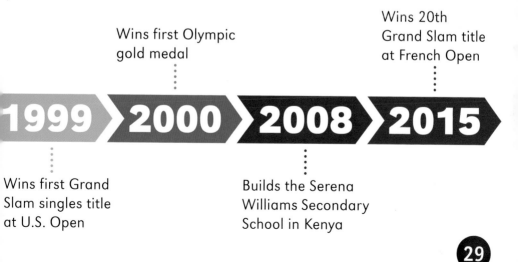

Wins first Olympic
gold medal

Wins 20th
Grand Slam title
at French Open

1999 > **2000** > **2008** > **2015**

Wins first Grand
Slam singles title
at U.S. Open

Builds the Serena
Williams Secondary
School in Kenya

A Poem About Serena Williams

A champion when on the court,
Serena plays to win.
And off the court, when helping out,
Serena is all in.

You Can Be a Champion

 Find something you love to do. Stick with it, and practice, practice, practice.

Ignore those who are against you for no reason; hold on to your beliefs.

Don't forget to give others a hand, too.

Glossary

ambassador (am-BASS-uh-dur): person sent by an organization to represent it

obstacles (AHB-stuh-kuhls): things that make it difficult to do or achieve something

perseverance (pur-suh-VEER-enss): continuing to do something even if it is hard or unlikely to succeed

racist (RAY-sist): unfair or cruel treatment based on race

Index

Facts for Now

Visit this Scholastic Web site for more information on Serena Williams:

www.factsfornow.scholastic.com

Enter the keywords Serena Williams

About the Author

Jodie Shepherd, who also writes under the name Leslie Kimmelman, is an award-winning author of dozens of books for children, both fiction and nonfiction. She is a huge tennis fan—but is far better at watching than playing.